To our adult readers,

There is a long tradition of using oral and written stories to share information and knowledge across generations. Many believe that within each of us is the power to heal and that stories have the ability to tap into our internal strength in an unconscious way. We are able to relate characters and plots to ourselves and to our lives. Therapeutic stories can be used to help children with any type of problem at any age. They are entertaining, engaging, and provide messages of love, power, and healing.

We recommend that this therapeutic story be read to young children nightly and that adults show patience in allowing the child to initiate any discussions of the content. If the child is quiet at the end of the book, then we suggest you close it and place it nearby until the next reading. When the child is ready, he or she might ask questions, share feelings, or identify with the elephant character. Your role can be to mirror back what the child is expressing and dispel any misconceptions or fears about the situation that caused the grief and loss. We advise against providing solutions or interpretations of your own.

If used in this manner, this book may even become a transitional object that represents hope and internal strength. We intentionally used a gender-neutral character and a whimsical look to attract all children to the story. We offered practical and realistic ideas for managing any type of grief and loss. Some children may have lost a pet while others may have lost a family member or been moved into foster care. Every child's experience with grief and loss is heartfelt and real.

Thank you for your care and dedication to the child that inspired you to obtain this book. We hope it helps!

Sincerely,

Amanda and Leslie

ISBN-13: 978-1492793243

THE ELEPHANT IN THE ROOM:

A CHILDRENS BOOK FOR GRIEF AND LOSS

THINGS MAY FEEL DIFFERENT,
AND THINGS HAVE CHANGED,

IT'S AS THOUGH THE WORLD
HAS BEEN REARRANGED

USE THESE KIND WORDS

TO HELP YOU ALONG THE WAY

AND REMEMBER OUR MEMORIES

ARE WITH YOU EVERYDAY

DRAW ME A PICTURE

OR WRITE ME A LETTER

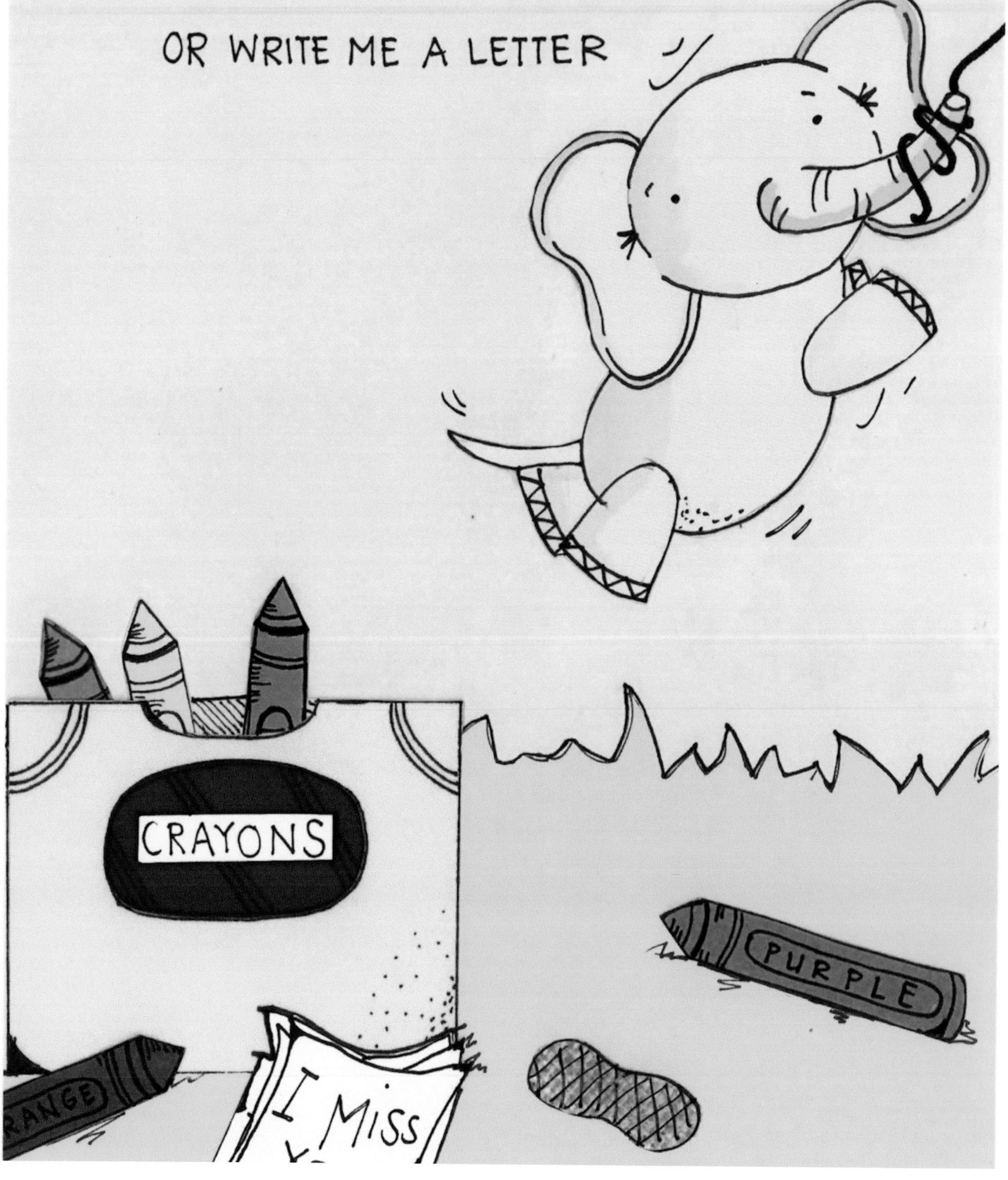

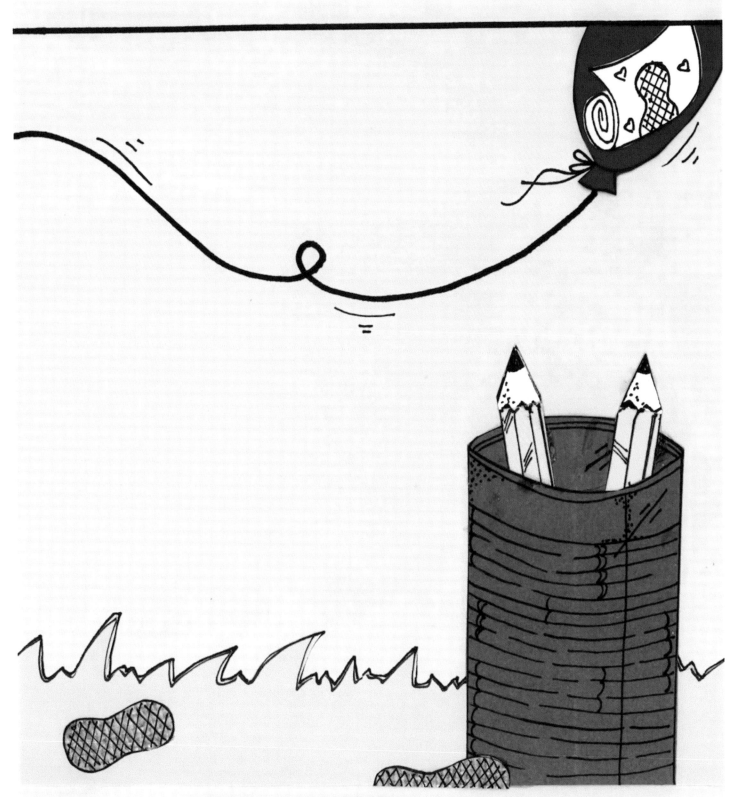

SEND IT AWAY

IN A BALLOON TO FEEL BETTER

IF YOU FEEL CONFUSED

OR JUST DON'T UNDERSTAND

ASK QUESTIONS, SEEK HELP

AND LET SOMEONE HOLD YOUR HAND

TAKE ME WHERE YOU CAN,

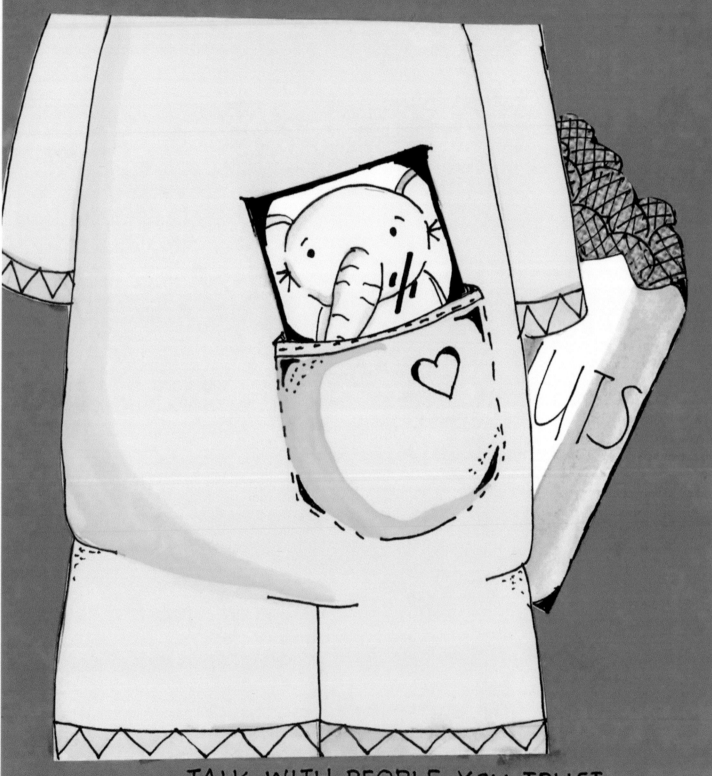

TALK WITH PEOPLE YOU TRUST

AND JUST REMEMBER

THAT MOVING ON IS NOT A RUSH

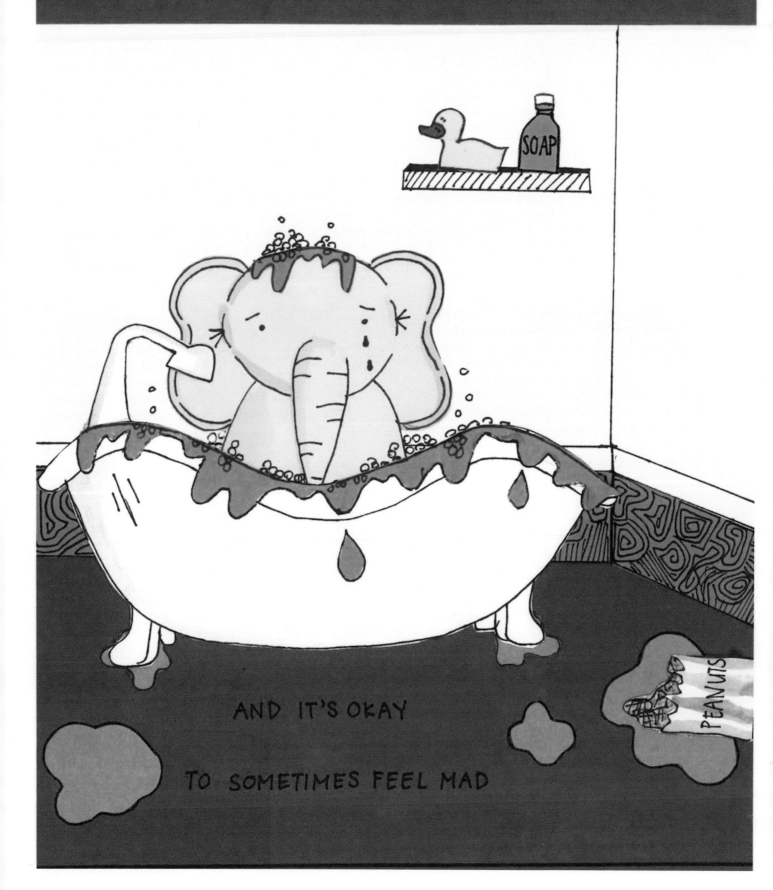

REMEMBER TO LET

THESE FEELINGS OUT

DON'T LET THEM BUILD UP

INTO AN EXPLOSIVE SHOUT

EMBRACE THOSE AROUND YOU,

EVEN IF THEIR HUGS MAY UPSET

AND REMEMBER THEIR THOUGHTS AND

INTENTIONS ARE NOT TO FORGET

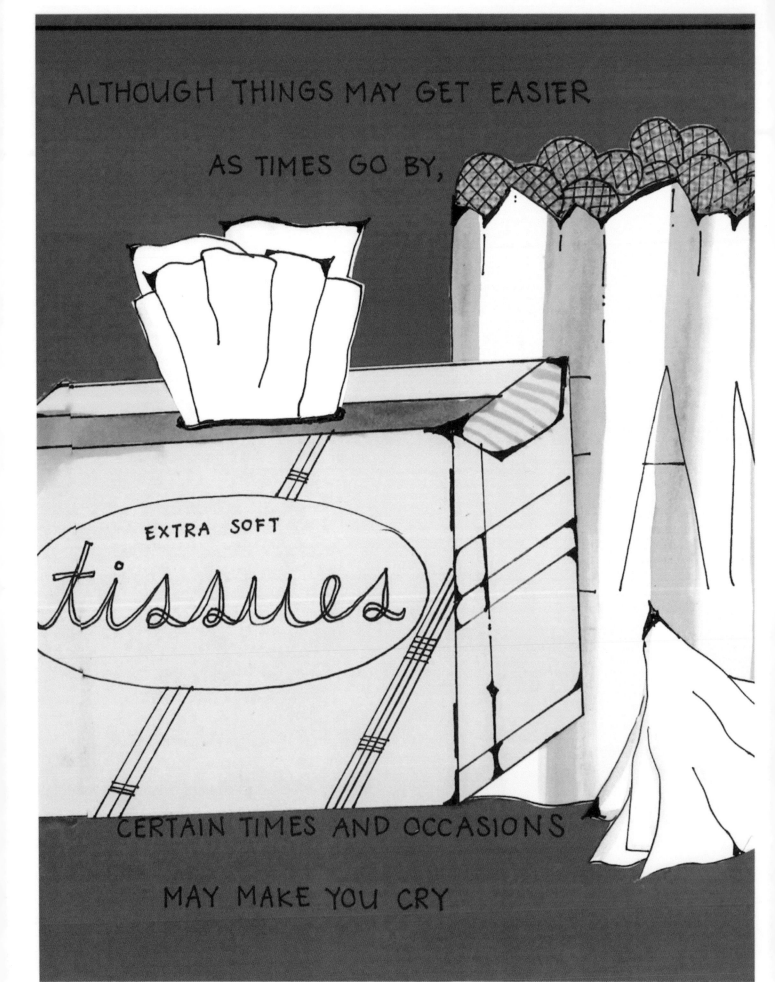

THIS NEW NORMAL MAY BE

DIFFICULT TO GRASP

BUT THESE FEELINGS

WILL SOON PASS

SO WHEN YOU FEEL ALONE

AND ALL YOU WANT TO DO IS CRY

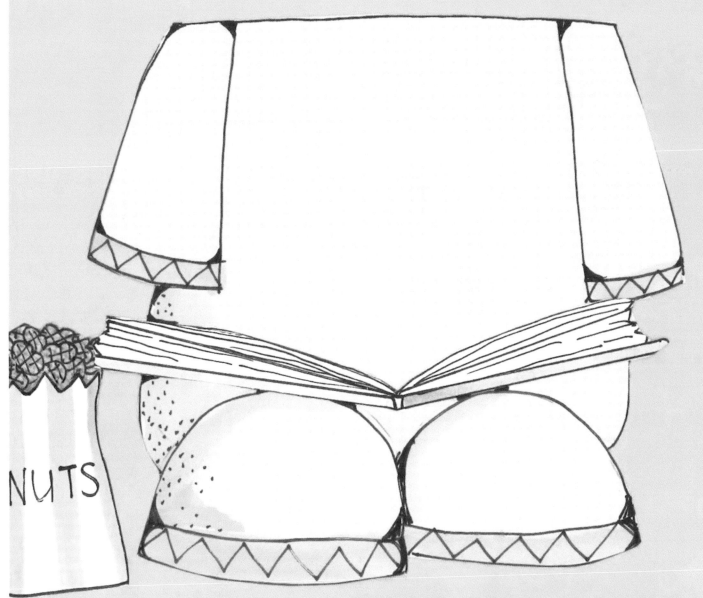

THINK OF THESE IDEAS

AND GIVE THEM A TRY

Amanda Edwards, M.A.
has been working in the field of early childhood education for the past 5 years. Her experience includes work with infants, toddlers, and preschool age children, in the education setting, as both a teacher and administrator. She currently holds a membership with the National Association for the Education of Young Children and recently completed her M.A. in early childhood education from Loyola Marymount University. Prior to her graduate work, she completed her B.A. in child and adolescent development with a minor in family studies from CSU, Northridge. Additionally, Amanda has volunteered as a research assistant studying inner-city foster youth, supported children in the hospital setting, and local community organizations. Her aspiration for early childhood education stems from her personal experiences, providing a strong passion to assist young children who experience grief and loss and their achievement of optimal development.

Leslie Ponciano, Ph.D.
is a developmental psychologist, a professor in Early Childhood Education at Loyola Marymount University, and a researcher examining the social and emotional development of children in non-parental care such as ECE classrooms and foster care. Prior to LMU, she taught Child Development at CSU, Los Angeles and Applied Developmental Psychology at UCLA. She has experience as a social worker/supervisor in foster care, an infant-toddler teacher, and a behavioral specialist. Dr. Ponciano serves on the Board of Directors for Peace4Kids, a community-based organization serving foster children, and is an advisor for ABCmouse.com, an online early learning academy. She has three children and was formerly a foster parent. Dr. Ponciano obtained a B.A. in Psychology from UCI, a M.A. in Developmental Psychology from Teachers College, Columbia University, and a Ph.D. in Psychological Studies in Education from UCLA.

Julia Horwitz
is a student at Vistamar High School with a love of writing and drawing, both in fine-point sharpie. In her past experience she has helped to orchestrate an arts summer program for students at an inner-city elementary school in Los Angeles. Her written work has been published in her school's literary magazine and newspaper and her artwork has been showcased at the Vistamar School Arts Night (It was at this showcase that Leslie Ponciano first came across her drawings). *The Elephant in the Room* is her first published illustrated work and has been an incredible experience.